Audra Pugh
Bethel #19 ♡ !!

Alexander

Alexandra Aurora

Job Schoeb
Jodie Bethel #25
to - Bee

Tyler

Guide '11

❤ I Love ❤ you

Lauren Garn
Bethel #25
Jr. Princess

Leia Garn
Bethel no.25
Sr. Princess

Live Long and
Prosper
Lia Ingersoll
#19 2011

Sarah
Librarian Thomas

Sarah Hallu
HBSP/HQ/PHQ #13

Tyler Parks
Bethel 25

Lyndie
Clifton
Bethel 19
11

Michaela Cook
PHQ, 8 Recorder
Bethel #25

Shelbie.B. Bethel 22

KATIE GAGA
Bethel no.19

Madeline Boisvert
Bethel #21
Choir

Jackie Hatton
Bethel 13

April Parks
HQ Bethel #25

Gabbi Dennis
Bethel 19
SB Rep to Delaware

Kayleigh Shaner
Bethel 13

Faith
Ryu
Bethel 14

Caroline Leidy
Bethel #11 ♡

Sarah Nutting
Bethel #22
Phoenix, AZ

MJ Baker
Bethel #22

Grace Fenimore
Bethel 25
Chaplin PHQ
We love you!!

Nice 2 meet u
Tabitha
T. :)

Megan Groves
Bethel 21 :)

Allie Louis
Bethel 13

Alyssa Houseman
Bethel 13

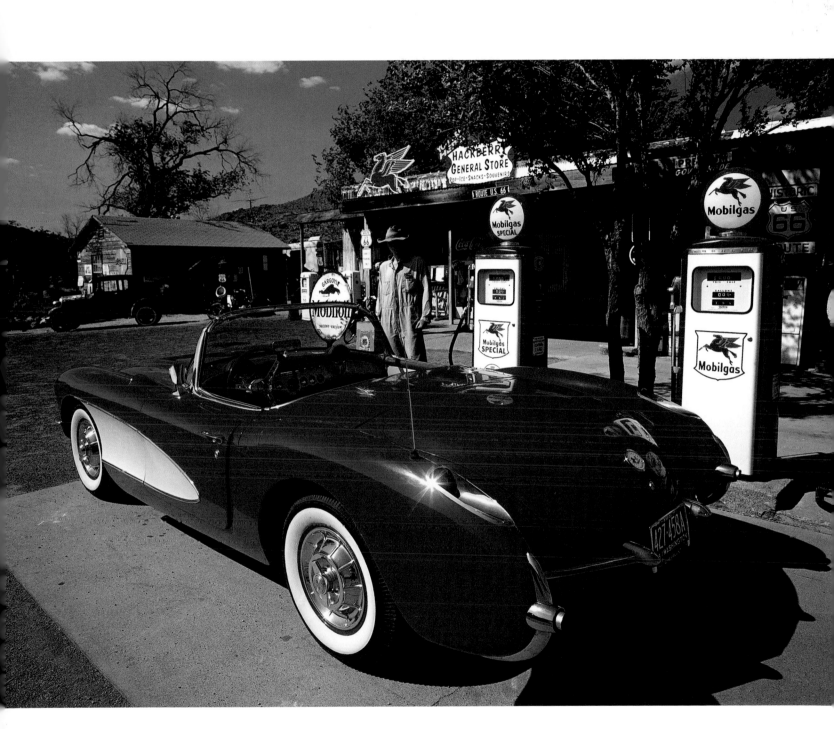

Our Arizona

Kerrick James

Voyageur Press

To my sons—Shane, Royce, and Keanu—who roam Arizona with me and give me reasons to roam anew.

First published in 2007 by Voyageur Press, an imprint of MBI Publishing Company LLC, Galtier Plaza, 380 Jackson Street, Suite 200, St. Paul, MN 55101 USA

Voyageur Press titles are also available at discounts in bulk quantity for industrial or sales-promotional use. For details write to Special Sales Manager at MBI Publishing Company, Galtier Plaza, 380 Jackson Street, Suite 200, St. Paul, MN 55101 USA.

To find out more about our books, join us online at www.VoyageurPress.com.

Library of Congress Cataloging-in-Publication Data

James, Kerrick.
  Our Arizona / Kerrick James.
    p. cm.
  ISBN-13: 978-0-7603-2837-8
  1. Arizona--Pictorial works. 2. Arizona--History, Local--Pictorial works. I. Title.
F812.J36 2007
979.1'0540222--dc22
                    2007018077

ON THE FRONT COVER: The sun-lit walls of the Grand Canyon reflect in the Little Colorado River near its confluence with the Colorado River.

ON THE BACK COVER: *(top)* The Phoenix skyline lights up in the evening, as seen here from South Mountain Park. *(center)* Horseback riders head through the North Window at Monument Valley Navajo Tribal Park. *(bottom left)* The Toroweap overlook provides a prime view of the Grand Canyon from atop a 3,000-foot cliff. *(bottom right)* Mission San Xavier del Bac, outside of Tucson, is known as the White Dove of the Desert.

ON THE SPINE: The sandstone Mittens glow in the late afternoon sun at Monument Valley.

PAGE 1: The last light of day settles on downtown Phoenix, as seen from Encanto Park.

PAGE 2: Hikers descend toward the Colorado River through the redwall limestone layer of the Grand Canyon.

PAGE 3: A light snow coats the high desert of Monument Valley, as viewed through Teardrop Arch.

PAGE 4: A slender stream carves its way through a White Mountains meadow en route to the Little Colorado River.

PAGE 5: An icon of the open road, a 1957 Corvette waits at the Hackberry General Store on Route 66.

TITLE PAGE: River runners and guides relax at the Anasazi granaries above Nankoweap, Grand Canyon National Park. *(inset)* A crescent moon hovers at sunset over saguaro cacti in South Mountain Park, Phoenix's largest city park and the largest municipal desert park in the world.

Editor: Josh Leventhal
Designer: Melissa Khaira

Printed in China

The silhouette of an agave lies in shadow below the landmark Zoroaster Temple at Grand Canyon National Park.

ABOVE

Wispy clouds caress the snowy walls of sedimentary rock above the Bright Angel Trail on a December morning at the Grand Canyon's South Rim.

RIGHT

Passing hikers trek along the upper section of the South Kaibab Trail in spring. The Kaibab Trail is a popular, and at times strenuous, path into the Grand Canyon.

TOP

River runners enjoy a game of baseball on a sandy "diamond" inside Redwall Cavern.

BOTTOM

A pair of sure-footed desert bighorn sheep amble along beside the Bright Angel Trail, just below the South Rim.

A faint rainbow appears in the stormy sunset light above Havasu Falls on the Havasupai Reservation.

ABOVE

Elves Chasm is a peaceful spot to rest and cool off while exploring the Grand Canyon.

RIGHT

Boaters pass through the narrow Muav Gorge in late afternoon on the Colorado River in Grand Canyon National Park.

ABOVE

The Desert View Watchtower offers a superb view at the end of the East Rim Drive in Grand Canyon National Park. The 70-foot-tall tower was built in 1932.

RIGHT

Architect Mary Colter incorporated elements from local tribes in her design for the Watchtower. Murals depicting traditional Hopi legends adorn this room on the first level.

Just south of Glen Canyon Dam near Page, the Colorado River takes a dramatic turn through the sandstone at Horseshoe Bend.

LEFT
Navajo weaver Mary Yazzie spins wool for rug making, near Page.

RIGHT
Hopi and Navajo artwork for sale at the Hubbell Trading Post National Historic Site, near Ganado. John Lorenzo Hubbell began trading with the Navajo here in the 1870s, and the Hubbell family continued to operate the trading post until the 1960s.

BELOW
The waters of Pipe Spring in northwestern Arizona have long attracted human settlers, from early Pueblo tribes to Mormons who built a ranch at the site. Today, re-enactors depict nineteenth century frontier life at Winsor Castle in Pipe Spring National Monument.

ABOVE

Over millions of years, the forces of wind, water, and erosion created sculpted formations of colored sandstone in the Paria Canyon–Vermilion Cliffs Wilderness Area in northern Arizona. The Wave, in the Coyote Buttes section of the Paria Plateau, is one of the most striking examples.

OPPOSITE PAGE, TOP

At the Moenave Formation west of Tuba City, dinosaur footprints are preserved in the ancient sandstone.

OPPOSITE PAGE, BOTTOM

The Tuba City Trading Post offers a wide selection of Native American arts, crafts, and souvenirs.

Dating from the Anasazi period, petroglyphs of flute-playing Kokopelli figures are etched in a sandstone wall at Monument Valley Navajo Tribal Park.

Chief Ray Tsosie, a Navajo tour guide, plays his flute in Cathedral Canyon, near Page. He is wearing a traditional Navajo rug in the "Two Grey Hills" pattern.

Antelope Canyon, outside of Page, is perhaps the most famous slot canyon in the American Southwest. Photographers, in particular, are drawn by the reflected sunlight on the sandstone's intriguing shapes and colors.

The sandstone glows red in the late afternoon sun at Monument Valley Navajo Tribal Park. This view of the twin buttes known as the Mittens and the neighboring Merrick Butte is an iconic image of the American Southwest.

ABOVE

Morning light casts shadows over the ochre wonderland of Monument Valley, viewed from the heights of Hunts Mesa.

LEFT

A crescent moon and Venus hang in the predawn sky above the Mittens. A nine-hour exposure reveals the tracks of the stars.

ABOVE

Spider Rock towers 800 feet above the canyon floor at Canyon de Chelly National Monument.

RIGHT

Ancient Puebloan tribes, or Anasazi, inhabited the canyons and rock walls of Canyon de Chelly for centuries. The White House Ruin, preserved inside an alcove at the base of a massive sandstone cliff, dates from between 1060 and 1275 AD.

RIGHT

A petrified tree stump stands vertical in front of Blue Mesa at Petrified Forest National Park.

LEFT

A petroglyph panel depicts male and female figures at Newspaper Rock in Petrified Forest National Park. Examples of this early art form can be found throughout the American Southwest.

BELOW

A sculpture below Window Rock pays tribute to the Navajo Code Talkers. The Code Talkers were Navajo soldiers who used their native language as a secret code to transmit messages for the U.S. armed forces, most notably during World War II.

ABOVE

Spring runoff from the White Mountains creates a torrent of muddy water at the Grand Falls of the Little Colorado River, northeast of Flagstaff.

LEFT

Monsoon rains bring out the rich colors of the badlands in Beautiful Valley, south of Chinle on the Navajo Reservation.

Sunrise light warms the volcanic landscape on Sunset Crater's eastern flank. The crater was formed by a series of volcanic eruptions beginning in the eleventh century. Today, Sunset Crater National Monument protects more than 3,000 acres surrounding the volcano.

About 40,000 to 50,000 years ago, a massive meteor hurtled through the atmosphere and struck the earth, creating a 4,000-foot-wide, 550-foot-deep pit in the Arizona plains. The impact of this meteorite is evident at Meteor Crater, east of Flagstaff.

OPPOSITE PAGE
A crescent moon rises above Wukoki Ruin, the best-preserved pueblo at Wupatki National Monument.

LEFT
The John Bushman home, built circa 1890, survives in Joseph City off of old Route 66. Bushman was a member of the early Mormon settlement here.

BELOW
Aspens in their autumn glory line the winding road to the Snowbowl ski area. The San Francisco Peaks rise in the background.

ABOVE

A full moon rises over the old downtown of Flagstaff. The landmark Weatherford Hotel, on the right, first welcomed guests in 1897.

PRECEDING PAGES

The Riordan brothers were prominent businessmen in Flagstaff during the early twentieth century. Their rustic yet luxurious home stands today as part of the Riordan Mansion State Historic Park.

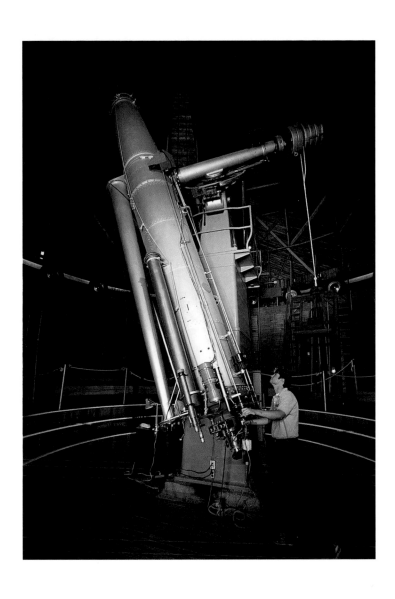

LEFT
The Clark telescope scans the night skies from Lowell Observatory in Flagstaff. The historic telescope was built in 1896.

BELOW
Upper St. Mary's Lake, southeast of Flagstaff, is a popular summertime destination for water-skiers and other watersports enthusiasts.

ABOVE

Red Rock Biplane Tours offers an exhilarating way to see the wilderness surrounding Sedona.

LEFT

Slide Rock State Park, in Oak Creek Canyon, provides a respite from the heat of Arizona summer days.

Schnebly Hill Road rises through the red rocks above Sedona to spectacular viewpoints and scenic campsites.

The Chapel of the Holy Cross, better known as the Red Rock Chapel, was built directly in the sandstone cliffs above Sedona.

Cathedral Rocks glow over Oak Creek in Red Rock Crossing State Park, west of Sedona.

A stormy spring sky overlays Sedona, as viewed from Airport Mesa.

LEFT

An eagle sits in its nest perched high above the Verde River in central Arizona.

BELOW

The Verde Canyon Railroad embarks from Clarkdale for a winding, forty-mile tour through Sycamore Canyon and other delights of the Verde Valley.

RIGHT

Prescott National Forest consists of more than a million acres of wilderness, including miles of hiking and mountain-biking trails.

BELOW

Climbers practice their skills on a granite island in Watson Lake, outside of Prescott.

LEFT
The Victorian-style Bashford House, built circa 1877, is one of nine historic structures at the Sharlot Hall Museum in Prescott.

The Palace Bar first opened on Prescott's Whiskey Row in 1877. The ornate 1880s-era Brunswick bar is still in use and evokes the town's frontier days.

LEFT
Bachelor officer's quarters were spartan indeed at Fort Verde, one of several nineteenth century army outposts on the Arizona frontier. Today the fort is preserved at Fort Verde State Historic Park.

BELOW
Jerome's famous sliding jail has moved nearly three hundred feet downhill in just over one hundred years.

Viewed through a vintage bubbled-glass window in the Flatiron Café across the street, the House of Joy in Jerome is a former brothel and restaurant. It currently operates as a gift shop.

ABOVE

Courage is on display every summer at the Payson Rodeo. Held every year since 1884, it is considered the oldest
continuous rodeo in the country.

OPPOSITE PAGE, TOP

A nineteenth-century schoolmarm oversees the 1885 schoolhouse in the village of Strawberry.

OPPOSITE PAGE, BOTTOM

Arcosanti, near Cordes Junction, was founded in 1970 by Italian architect Paolo Soleri as an experimental community
under the concept of arcology (a merging of architecture and ecology). Arcosanti's famous cast-bronze bells are available
for purchase and help fund the project.

ABOVE
Horses graze at a ranch north of Skull Valley.

RIGHT
A hiker goes bouldering under the limestone layers of the Tonto Natural Bridge, purportedly the world's largest natural travertine bridge.

ABOVE

The rugged peaks of Superstition Mountain have inspired wonder and curiosity for centuries, from the native Pima tribes to early European settlers. Saguaros dot the landscape below the western front of the mountain, as viewed from Lost Dutchman State Park.

LEFT

The *Dolly* steamboat offers sightseeing cruises on scenic Canyon Lake east of Phoenix.

Morning light illuminates the ruins of an ancient Salado Indian settlement within the cliffs of Rogers Canyon in the Superstition Mountain Wilderness Area.

LEFT

Off-road adventurers explore the Sonoran Desert after a rare spring snowfall in the Superstition Mountains.

ABOVE

Two brothers look out over the Valley of the Sun from Hole-in-the-Rock at Papago Park, Phoenix.

LEFT

Colorful flowers blanket the slopes of Lost Dutchman State Park in spring. The park earned its name from a lost gold mine allegedly discovered by German immigrant Jacob Waltz.

Putting on the fourth hole of the Dinosaur Mountain Course in Gold Canyon.

Hikers descend the Piestewa Peak Summit Trail in Phoenix's Piestewa Peak Park.

South Mountain Park offers sprawling views of downtown Phoenix and the surrounding mountains.

A hawk soars from a saguaro cactus near the Superstition Wilderness.

Completed in 1900—twelve years before Arizona was granted statehood—the grand Arizona State Capitol building is topped by a copper dome and Winged Victory statue. The state legislature moved to adjacent modern offices in 1960, and the restored original building now operates as a museum.

A mosaic of the state seal of Arizona is set in the floor of the Arizona State Capitol.

The historic Rosson House, circa 1895, is an Eastlake-style Victorian in downtown Phoenix.

Regular-season baseball came to Arizona with the formation of the Diamondbacks in 1998. The team's home park is Chase Field, a state-of-the-art facility with a retractable roof in downtown Phoenix.

RIGHT

Nearly 75,000 fans pack Sun Devils Stadium in Tempe to cheer on the ASU football team in a game against USC.

ABOVE

A perfect day for baseball at the Oakland A's spring training field, Phoenix Municipal Stadium. Arizona hosts the spring training facilities for more than a dozen Major League Baseball clubs.

OPPOSITE PAGE

Outdoor chess anyone? The Arizona Biltmore Resort & Spa in Phoenix features an oversized chess board among its many luxurious amenities. The hotel was built in 1929 based on designs inspired by Frank Lloyd Wright.

Built in 1937, Taliesin West in Scottsdale was the winter home of legendary architect Frank Lloyd Wright. It continues to operate as the winter home of the architectural school and as the headquarters for the Frank Lloyd Wright Foundation.

Phoenix's Burton Barr Central Library is an architectural wonder in the desert.

Designed as a work of art itself, the Nelson Fine Arts Center on the campus of Arizona State University in Tempe features impressive art within its galleries.

LEFT
This all-American cowboy boot is public art on display in Old Town Scottsdale.

RIGHT
A saguaro cactus on Chandler Boulevard brings a little Christmas cheer to the desert city of Phoenix.

BELOW
A creatively designed cardboard bus-boat floats in Tempe Town Lake during the city's annual Great Cardboard Boat Regatta.

ABOVE

Jack Knife, by Ed Mell, adorns the gallery district in Old Town Scottsdale.

PRECEDING PAGES

Christmas lights are a traditional delight at the Mesa Arizona Temple. Built in 1927, it is one of the largest Mormon temples.

The Mesa Arts Center is aglow at twilight. It is one of Arizona's largest exhibition and performance spaces for the performing and visual arts.

A bearded dragon lizard soaks up the sun at the Phoenix Zoo. More than 1,200 animals are on exhibit at the zoo's 125-acre grounds in Papago Park.

A Tyrannosaurus Bataar menaces at the Mesa Southwest Museum.

Boyce Thompson Arboretum is Arizona's largest and oldest botanical garden. Some 3,200 desert plants are on display, including specialized collections like a hummingbird garden, a cactus garden, a eucalyptus forest, and more.

Golden barrel cacti are among the hundreds of cactus, succulent, and other desert species that flourish at the Desert Botanical Garden in Phoenix.

A waterfall in Mescal Creek in the Needle's Eye Wilderness provides cool refreshment on a hot summer day. Mescal Creek is a tributary of the Gila River.

ABOVE

Goldfield was a booming gold-mining town in the 1890s before fading into ghost-town status. Today, it is a popular tourist attraction, with re-enactors depicting life in the Old West.

LEFT

The Big House, constructed of adobe, is the centerpiece of Casa Grande Ruins National Monument. The structure was built by the Hohokam people approximately 700 years ago.

The second Pinal County Courthouse, built circa 1891, stands near the center of town in Florence.

Mission San Xavier del Bac was first established by Jesuit priest Eusebio Francisco Kino in 1700. The first two churches on the site were destroyed, and the current building dates from the 1790s.

Fires light up the night during the Spring Historic Festival at Mission San Xavier del Bac.

LEFT

With a recently restored interior, Mission San Xavier del Bac still serves the Tohono O'odham San Xavier Indian Reservation.

BELOW

Tin flowers decorate the entryway to the DeGrazia Gallery in the Sun in Tucson. The gallery celebrates the life and work of local artist Ettore "Ted" DeGrazia, who died in 1982.

LEFT
A mural of outlaws covers a wall in Tucson.

BELOW
The chapel in the DeGrazia Gallery in the Sun, known as the Mission in the Sun, features colorful murals depicting the life and faith of the local people.

Cactus plants frame the doorways of an adobe dwelling in the Barrio Historico District of Tucson.

LEFT

A coyote is alert and watchful at the Arizona-Sonora Desert Museum in Tucson. The Arizona-Sonora Desert Museum is a combination zoo, natural history museum, and botanical garden that presents innovative programs about the ecology and life of the desert.

RIGHT

A forest of saguaro cacti flourishes on a south-facing slope at Gates Pass near Tucson.

BELOW

Summer clouds hover over the Santa Catalina Mountains and downtown Tucson. Known as the "Old Pueblo," Tucson is one of the fastest growing cities in the United States.

TOP

A rattlesnake slithers to cover just off the Fort Bowie Trail in the Chiricahua Mountains of southeastern Arizona.

BOTTOM

A spectacular crested saguaro is stunning to behold in Organ Pipe National Monument.

LEFT

The hedgehog cactus' dainty pink blossoms contrast with its sharp spines following a spring rain.

ABOVE

Sun lovers are drawn to the Sabino Canyon Recreation Area during the summer to cool off in the waters below Seven Falls. Sabino Canyon lies in the foothills of the Santa Catalina Mountains outside of Tucson.

LEFT

A hiker descends through spring snow on the Red Ridge Trail in the Santa Catalina Mountains northwest of Tucson.

The Chiricahua Mountains hold a rich diversity of plant and animal life. Cave Creek Canyon, on the eastern side of the mountains, is a birders' paradise.

ABOVE

Horseback riders enjoy a morning ride across the grasslands of the San Rafael Valley, southeast of Patagonia.

RIGHT

Baxter Black, the renowned cowboy poet, "thinks stuff up" by a twilight campfire near Mescal in a classic Southwestern scene.

LEFT

The grave marker for Little Robe, a son of Apache chief Geronimo, is found just off the trail to Fort Bowie National Historic Site.

BELOW

The adobe walls of the cavalry barracks still stand at Fort Bowie National Historic Site, which commemorates the fierce battle between the U.S. Army and the Chiricahua Apaches here in July 1862. U.S. troops waged war against the Apaches in the region for more than twenty years.

False fronts and boardwalks still line Allen Street in historic Tombstone, evoking the town's Wild West heritage.

OPPOSITE PAGE, TOP

OPPOSITE PAGE, TOP

The Tombstone Courthouse State Historic Park houses many exhibits that explore life in nineteenth century Tombstone, as well as a famous gallows.

OPPOSITE PAGE, BOTTOM

Still printing, the Tombstone *Epitaph* tells the news of the day, though not every day.

RIGHT

Citizen Moore found immortality the hard way at Boot Hill in Tombstone.

BELOW

The famous OK Corral gunfight is re-enacted daily in Tombstone.

RIGHT

The Shady Dell Trailer Park in Bisbee offers unique accommodations in vintage trailers decked out in period style, such as this 1954 Crown.

LEFT

The neon sign outside Benson's Horse Shoe Cafe reflects the eatery's Western decor and ambiance.

ABOVE

Guests at the historic Gadsden Hotel in the border city of Douglas are greeted by a luxurious art deco lobby adorned with stained glass windows, marble staircase and columns, and gold-leaf decoration.

S. Grant Sergot checks out a "Tom Mix" hat at his Optimo Hatworks in Bisbee.

ABOVE

Poppies color the hillside above the old copper-mining town of Bisbee.

RIGHT

A sculpture in Bisbee pays tribute to the town's copper miners.

The remnants of an ore chute survive near Washington Camp, just north of the Mexican border.

Adobe walls meld into the soil of Gleeson, a copper-mining ghost town south of the Dragoon Mountains.

Grapes decorate the Arizona Vineyards winery east of Nogales. This mountainous region of southeastern Arizona is home to as many as half a dozen wineries.

History guards the graves at Mission San José de Tumacácori. The Tumacácori National Historical Park preserves the adobe ruins of three Spanish colonial missions in the Santa Cruz Valley: Tumacácori, Guevavi, and Calabazas.

Mexican girls dance in the December sun during the annual La Fiesta de Tumacácori at Tumacácori National Historical Park.

OPPOSITE PAGE

A scorching July day steals over Blackbird Island and the Bill Williams River National Wildlife Refuge. The refuge protects a rare ecosystem of cottonwood-willow forest along the lower Colorado River.

LEFT

Lake Havasu City's London Bridge is one of the state's most popular attractions. In 1968, the historic bridge was dismantled in London and shipped to Arizona, where it was reassembled over a manmade canal.

BELOW

In summertime, boaters cruise the waters of the Colorado River, and the river's shores are packed with campers and RVers, as seen here north of the city of Parker.

LEFT

More than three thousand prisoners were held behind bars at the Yuma Territorial Prison from 1876 to 1909.

RIGHT

Canoers explore Emerald Cave in the Black Canyon on the Colorado River.

BELOW

The historic Ocean to Ocean Bridge crosses the Colorado River in Yuma.

ABOVE
You can sleep in a teepee with a TV at the Wigwam Motel in Holbrook, on historic Route 66.

OPPOSITE PAGE, TOP LEFT
Route 66 is a true American icon. Vestiges of the old road can be found across Arizona, from Oatman near the California border to Holbrook in the east.

OPPOSITE PAGE, TOP RIGHT
During the annual Cool Country Cruise-In rally, classic cars line the streets of downtown Williams, along the path of old Route 66.

OPPOSITE PAGE, BOTTOM
The longest intact stretch of Route 66 runs through Kingman, and the town plays up its connections to the "Mother Road."

ABOUT THE AUTHOR

Kerrick James has been a professional photographer for more than twenty years. He moved to Arizona in 1990, and since that time he has specialized in travel imagery. He is a regular contributor to Getty Images; Arizona Highways, Sunset, and National Geographic Adventure magazines; and the magazine for Alaska Airlines. He also provided the color photography for *Backroads of Arizona* (Voyageur Press, 2006). Kerrick lives in Mesa with his three sons.

To create the photos that appear in this book, Kerrick used Pentax film and digital cameras, with the exception of the panoramic images. The 35mm cameras—used primarily to capture action, people, and wildlife—were the Pentax LX, PZ-1P, and MZ-S. The landscapes were shot with the Pentax 67II, for maximum quality. Digital image capture was made using the Pentax *ist D and the K10D. Lenses used ran from 10mm to 600mm for digital capture; 17mm to 600mm for 35mm film format; and 35mm full-frame fish-eye to 300mm for the 6x7cm medium format.

Kerrick's films of choice are Fuji Velvia 50, Fuji Velvia 100, and Kodak E-100 VS. These are richly saturated, contrasty films with a narrow exposure latitude. He also selectively used normal and warming polarizing filters and graduated neutral density and warming filters. Digital image processing was accomplished using Adobe Photoshop CS2 on MAC G5 systems.

Jackie
Graham
Bethel #22
duece-duece
love you! xoxoxo

Breanne
Mueller ♡
LOVE ♡
Bethel #22

Thank you for coming
to campout! It was
so nice meeting you!
♡ Erin Dye #41

Jea Lynn Scott
Bethel # 22
We love you!!

Suzanne
Kilday
bethel #22

~ Thanks for
coming to our
campout ~

Love
Taylor
Bellamy
"Deuce · Deuce"

Ashley YHQ
Fuller Bethel
#11 ♡
Jobie Love

Than
For
Tes

Thanks for
coming out to AZ!
- Kaileigh Walker
JMAJD (Bethel 19)

Shannon Oju
Bethel # 21
Chaplin

Thank you
for visiting!
We ♡ you! xoxo
:) ~Heather
Peterson
Bethel 19

Bethell # 19
Stephanie Lewis

Samantha
Roebuck
Bethel #11 ♥